T0077384

Epics

Of

Man

Freddie McSears Jr.

Order this book online at www.trafford.com
or email orders@trafford.com

Most Trafford titles are also available at major online book retailers.

Printed in the United States of America.

ISBN: 978-1-4269-0377-9 (sc)
ISBN: 978-1-4269-0378-6 (e)

Trafford rev. 7/15/2009

 www.trafford.com
North America & international
toll-free: 1 888 232 4444 (USA & Canada)
fax: 812 355 4082

Foreword

March 10, 2000. The news of my father's passing hit me like a ton of bricks. At the time, I wasn't really sure why. I mean, we were not particularly close. Hadn't I spent years mourning his absence? Looking for love in all the wrong places and coming up short?

The longings I experienced as a child as a result of his absence eventually blended into the normal everyday sorrows of life as I emerged as a young woman and I thought I had done pretty well for myself without him. But when I learned that he was gone at the age of 59…that he died of "pending" causes in a rooming house alone, I was engulfed with a wave of sorrow that I was not prepared to handle. Without knowing how to reconcile what I was feeling, I tucked away the pain and continued living.

However, when I read, Epics of a Man, the familiar emotions I experienced when my father died revisited me. But this time, I wasn't scared of being swept away by the sorrow. As I read Freddie's dedication to his son, Joshua, I vicariously experienced what if feels like to be blessed by a father and to have that discerning father care enough to anticipate questions I would have about myself and about him and have those answers revealed in a memoir.

Through the safety of the pages, the little girl within me, who had been silent for so many years, emerged. Her tears stained the pages as she cried for moments missed and time wasted. So many questions left unanswered, like: What were your hopes for me? How did you survive Vietnam? Why did you drink? What kind of man should I marry? Did you love my mom? How come the two of you could not stay married and work things out? When you and my mother divorced, why didn't you fight to be apart of my life? What's the greatest thing that ever happened to you? Were you proud of me? Did you love me?...

Just as fathers validate the identity of their sons, fathers also establish and safeguard the value of their daughters. The tragedy of my father's death, that I could not articulate some eight years earlier, is that he lived and died without establishing my value, without making himself accessible to me to provide answers to my questions, and without extending his blessing of provision and protection over my life. Yet, as I read through the pages of Epics of a Man, Freddie's humanity, transparency, and honesty helped me to finally realize the importance of holding onto the good, letting go of the bad, and of allowing God's love, grace, mercy, and forgiveness to wash over and heal my broken heart and wounded spirit.

As you read this powerful collection of poems, housed in a memoir to Joshua, the potential exists for a deeply profound and personal experience. If you are like me and have grown up without the benefit of your father, may you experience the tenderness and strength of a father's love? If you are a father, young or old, and you have failed to make yourself and your life accessible to your children, may this work compel you to reach out to your children? If you have failed to extend or have withheld your blessing, may this piece inspire you to find a way to establish the value of your daughters and to authenticate the identity of your sons. For those, who experienced loving and nurturing relationships with their fathers, may this work fill you with the kind of compassion that will lead you to care for, embrace, and protect the fatherless.

This is a book of poetry about mature themes written uniquely by Freddie McSears Jr. to share sensitive issues with his son.   Its purpose is to stimulate thought, discussion and questions as to the origin of the information. Above all, may this memoir, a natural display of a father's love for his son, lead you into a deeper and more personal revelation of the Father's love for you and for me?

Philicia Corine Randolph, M.A.

Dedication To Joshua

I dedicate this to my son, Joshua Izaiah McSears. My child when I first learned of your arrival I was confused; surprised and concerned about the life you were about to enter into. Through your creation the instability remained constant and the concern for you did not change. As it became clear on your arrival into this world your strength started to show. Your energy, responsiveness and temperament emerged while you were still in the womb.

As I looked into your eyes many things began to happen. First, you stared without blinking and I wondered what could possibly be wrong. Second, after your initial cry, you were silent unless provoked to make noise. Third, I felt you communicated with me by your stare and established through your innocence that you would make it through adversity. You were truly the most beautiful creation I had ever seen. Initially overwhelmed by your presence I had to gain composure of myself. As your father I will do everything I can to empower, motivate, encourage and provide protection for you no matter what the circumstances.

My dear son, your thirst for life comes through in your presence. You are a leader among people and will have a life that will yield many challenges, which you will overcome. You are intelligent, strong and stubborn. Your stubbornness will not inhibit your performance, but will propel you to stand up for yourself and others. You will fear God and exercise faith that will encourage you to remain grounded.

Everyone you meet will not like you, but you will command respect by all you encounter. You will be hurt and you will survive it through the power of forgiveness. You will not be exploited though some will try to convince you of their lies. Live strong with a righteous spirit. Seek your own truth and do not follow a lost soul, ever.

Make certain you are aware of who you have around you because some will try to use your presence to bring value to their existence. Do not have any guilt because of this; their choices have created their path, which you are beyond. I will work to help you empower your life and I advise you to surround yourself by people who will encourage your confidence when it is lacking. You must use information combined with your spirit and heart to choose your path.

Do not ever allow any human being to make you feel bad for wanting to be good. It is important you understand with integrity of labor success is inevitable. Simply stated, there is no short cut to achievement, with hard work, discipline and teamwork a sincere effort will yield prosperity every time.

Furthermore, surround yourself by those you can learn from with attributes that contribute to a worthy purpose. You are loved and protected by a father, daddy, guide, counselor, guardian and educator who continue to beat the odds. I thank God for you, daily.
My dear son, I will be there for you always.

Freddie McSears Jr.

When I started this I did not anticipate releasing it. Some call this a collection of poems or short stories. To me, they are thoughts and experiences I was able to convey into words. Enjoy and Be Encouraged.

Contents

Steps In Life
1

Facets Of Love
23

Steps

In

Life

My Joshua

Being of sound mind and body I ponder my thoughts of
you,
Not knowing what in this life will you do?
Your conception was not my plan,
Never doubt I will take a stand to intercede for you and fill
the gaps until you are ready to fill them on your own.

I will not abandon you, nor will I leave your side,
At times when it seems I am far away because of where I
reside, I am still with you.
You will have my love and support but the price will be your
focus and effort in life's endeavors.
My love does not require payment, but if God who you
cannot see has standards, rests assure I who you can see have
them.

I seek to be not laboring in vain,
In your absence I endure such pain because at times, we are
apart.
There are no secrets to life; the only secrets will be the ones
you keep inside of yourself.

Open your mind and soul to learn as much as you can, in
addition, protect yourself from corrupt information.
Those you choose to have around you will not decide your
fate, but they will influence your actions.

Maturity and strength will help guide your thoughts to actions of integrity and courage.

Most good leaders are first followers, whom you choose to follow will dictate your future.

CHOOSE WISELY !!!!

Coming of Age

As I open my eyes to the start of a lifetime,
I am overwhelmed with dreams of aspirations.
One must crawl to walk, and slowly learn to run, with each
step of effort comes freedom to explore.
With the innocence of a new heart, with lack of shyness, life
appears to be an open book to read.
Everything comes easy because the world evolves around
all of my needs and I make noise to get attention without
consequence.
To further display my control I can release my waste and
have the privilege of being sanitized as often as I choose.
Then my eyes close for rest,
My soul, mind and body endures the test,
I grow long and strong to wake again.
What am I ?

As I open my eyes on the verge of adulthood,
I learn the importance of setting goals,
One realizes that setting standards does not mean
maintaining or surpassing them.
The pains of mistakes are recoverable.
The thirst for challenge and change is an inferno that rages
with the intensity of an erupting volcano.
I feel invincible; because I can recklessly eat and maintain
firm physical stamina, in addition, make love endlessly
without fatigue.

I know everything and whoever does not agree with me is wrong because I am ready to take on the world.
Strength, endurance and action from youth are the fuel that feeds my fire to affect everything around me.
Then my eyes close for rest,
My soul, mind and body endures the test,
I grow long and strong to wake again.
What am I ?

As I open my eyes to what my choices have made me, I am confused about what I see.
Am I what I am meant to be, less or more?
I measure what I see by what I know compared to what I believe.
If these thoughts are consistent with one another, I am pleased.
I have a title and money or lack there of.
My life illustrates a picture that is detailed with delicate lines.
I look ahead to a pension and relaxation, with luck, both.
My legacy is important, I don't want to be forgotten, but what part of me will remain in my absence.

I want to stay I am not finished, I don't know if I have begun.
I move slower and my body occasionally fails me, but I have the wisdom of a lifetime.
My eyes are heavy, I have faith, but as my eyes close, I don't want to remain in darkness.
I want the color of life to surround me forever.
I want to live; I want to live.
Then my eyes close for rest,

My soul, mind and body endures the test,
I grow long and strong to wake again in another place.
What am I ?

Sunset

What's in a sunset?
A smile, frown or is it your ambiance that leads to the
comfort of your touch.
What's in a sunset?
Is it color, a rainbow or the sweetness of your smile I love so
much?
What's in a sunset?
Is it peace or war, or the fresh sensation of a new start?
What's in a sunset?
Is it the barrier that keeps us so far apart?
What's in a sunset?
Is it the end or beginning of what is to come?
What's in a sunset?
Is it a shape or amoeba that forms to resemble the birth of
the sun?
What's in a sunset?
Is it the problem I had to endure yesterday or maybe the
disappointment of not getting my way?
What's in a sunset?
The darkness of night as it fades to black.
What's in a sunset?
The stillness of my shadow with qualities I lack.
What's in a sunset?
As I sit and think of you, wondering if you are thinking of
me too.

What's in a sunset?
I look closely to see reflections of me.
As we all look, it's whatever you want it to be.

A sunset holds treasures for us all,
No matter how large or how small,
If we don't see it, we feel it,
If we don't feel it, we still know it's there to remind us of the
end or beginning…
Regardless, don't fear the night, within it, you may find your
light.

Treasures in A Clay Jar

With each step comes more space taking me further than
before,
It is my goal not to go back wishing I had more
(information), that is,
Life is not a script to live by,
Therefore I must proceed because soon I will surely die.
I try to learn as much as I can,
As I face this life as a strong man,
My journey goes from one place to another,
At times I struggle, similar to that of others,
I just don't know how to find what I am looking for,
A guide is what I need to find my treasures for sure,
Why it seems lost within me,
God open my eyes so I can see.

Is it near or is it far,
I am looking for my treasure in this clay jar.

My experience is all I have to go on, but I get lost in what it
means,
I follow the path as I have been taught and I still get lost in
my dreams,
Here I go, off on a tangent confusing you,
All I want is to understand what I am here to do,
I move through this journey to locate the gift,
Wondering if I am meant to find it or am I chasing a myth.

Is it near or is it far,
I am looking for my treasure in this clay jar.

In frustration I often fall short of standards in my mind,
Does anyone also have these thoughts of a similar kind?
As life has continued, it's amazing to know what life others see,
As time settles into years,
Often do you think of what you hear?
What am I to do with the time I have left?
Sit, walk, move quickly or place myself on a shelf and wait, afraid to move.

Is it near or is it far,
I am looking for my treasure in this clay jar.

To not lose sight of where I plan to go,
I will try to explain this scenario,
The steps that I take and the places I see are facets of where I need to be.
I live life with no map to travel,
Going through my journey hoping this life does not unravel,
We all have gifts given by a divine force,
I struggle to locate them and not have remorse.
I don't know what talent I have to give, but I know I must continue to live.

These treasures I speak of are gifts from above,
This clay jar I speak about, is my soul, body and mind that I love.
I want to discover my gifts inside of me,
To give to those who choose to listen intently.

Is it near or is it far,
I am looking for my treasure in this clay jar.

Late Bloomer

June was a time that has come and gone,
In sadness and joy I wonder what went wrong.
Twenty years of living and striving to gain,
As I reflect to humbly subdue the pain.
You see life has been fairly good to me,
But when I look in the mirror what do I see.
Success and failure as I measure my worth,
Living in the sky to pay bills on earth.
When is it enough how much do I earn?
Before I truly determine what I need to learn.
My brother I have placed a mountain in front of me,
Now why? Is a question I will have to answer?
What will become of this wall to climb?
Will I fall or break my head.
No I will not fall and die,
It's time to reach for the sky.
I make a living through the clouds,
I did not place a mountain in front of me,
But it was God who did it you see.

He said you have been fighting to succeed alone, though you
have talent as you have grown.
Don't keep what I gave you to yourself,
Go get your brother's to discover your wealth.
Hold each other's hand and pull one another along,
Then and only then will you be strong.

Maybe we should have done this sooner,
It's better late than never,
Get ready to be a late bloomer.

It's time to groove on my friend with love, power, focus,
precision, and creativity as we strive for the goodness in life.
I have my will and so do you,
But together with our crew, what can we do.
To climb the mountain alone, I don't know if I can do it,
But together we can go straight through it.
Maybe we should have done this sooner,
It's better late than never,
Get ready to be a late bloomer.

Keep your ears, spirit and mind open with the strength to
keep your mouth shut.
Look not for success from the work, but for the love in the
work and success will take care of itself.
Einstein said; "Helping people do better in their lives is the
greatest of all achievements."
A little something from the certainty of the unknown,
Are you ready to bloom like spring in the winter, I am.

Raise the Bar

Who would have thought coming from my town,
I would be the one to get out to get down.
With beats in a measure with space to move,
Flowing through melodies with a hypnotic groove.
When I was young I wanted so much to be a man,
Trying to learn what I did not know, life was so hard to
comprehend.

Many lessons came the hard way,
On occasions I did not know whether to run or stay to fight
another day.
Grade school was a blur because there were so many,
I am at nine and counting it's all a distant memory.
I tried to pay attention to what elder's would say,
It was so difficult because I did not want their life anyway.
I did not consider myself better or worse,
I was held accountable for what I did not know, that was my
curse.

I don't seek a star,
But I now know to survive I have to raise the bar.
It does not matter how near or far,
To sustain the life I live I must raise the bar.

I live as a young man striving to learn more,
Life has not given me riches galore.
I don't settle for the complacency in a comfort zone,
But I will not forget the lessons of home.
Praise and attention I don't need,
But respect is one thing I demand indeed.
I don't ask for what I can't give,
I sure wish that were how other's lived.
Sometimes this life is not easy.

I don't seek a star,
But I now know to survive I have to raise the bar.
It does not matter how near or far,
To sustain the life I live I must raise the bar.

So much time was spent seeking words,
It's funny how I hardly remember what I heard.
Finally, late in August I became aware,
I found some of us really care.
To be perfect within a groove is real and alive,
The trick is to be prepared when it arrives.
It comes and goes,
Sometimes fast at other times slow.
The truth is in all of us.
We simply have to seek what is real beneath the disguise of
negative people.

Bailey told me if I read the good, I must read the bad,
I don't think he knows the effect he had.
Miles above the earth I make my living,
Still with love I keep on giving.
You see these days, some people stare,

It took Nature/Bass to make me aware,
Of what I had inside of me all this time.

I still don't seek a star,
But I will continue to raise the bar.
Like a sweet touchdown in a strong crosswind,
I must takeoff to prove myself over and over again.

Sie La Vie

And life goes on.

Penetrating Influence

Once again I sit on a cloud watching the sunset,
I ride west leaving the night behind me,
As I move forward with the wind in my face,
I ponder the fate within my destiny.

How do I adjust to the life ahead?
Do I give up, give in or stand,
With many things out of my control,
I don't know if I have anyone sincere about offering a helping
hand.

People talk of what they will do,
With their own lives full of broken dreams,
Why is it judgments are made of me?
A million pieces of one lie or so it seems.

I go through the paces hoping for the best,
To my own admission I wonder if this is a test from God to
stretch me beyond my limits.
Whether I do soul searching or soul stretching I am lost,
Moving forward to the sun,
Wow…this is an unusual one.

Trying to make sense of my life causes me so much
confusion,
The more logic and thought, the more fragmented pieces that
need to be mended together.

People talk of what they will do,
With their own lives full of broken dreams,
Why is it judgments are made of me?
A million pieces of one lie or so it seems.

Still moving forward as day turns into night,
Usually doing wrong while knowing what's right,
Is it real or a dream as I focus on what has become of me in
this world at this time and place?
With trials of change constantly in my face,
One never knows what comes next,
Do I make an adjustment or become fixed on the here and
now?
To make a decision is something I do not fear,
The significance of this is to live with my conscience
regardless…
It's funny; on occasions I hear a small voice, to remind me to
make a quality choice.

People talk of what they will do,
With their own lives full of broken dreams,
Why is it judgments are made of me?
A million pieces of one lie or so it seems.
I am so challenged by this life I live,
My heart beats with the rhythm of my soul and the groove
goes on because I refuse to die overcome by my decisions.
My life is my own, but the purpose is from the ONE who
sent me.

Life in A Moment of
A Decision

The factors of life that effect my love for you are few,
A pillar of strength I will always be standing right next to you.
Consumed in doing what is right to protect us,
I'm caught up in the dilemma of choosing between love and lust,
I spend so much time building bridges for us to cross,
Epitomizing the road to travel not to get lost on the other side.
I often look and wonder, "Who is the blame?"
The answer is, "No One," my choices good or bad are accepted without malice or shame.
Whether we are similar or have different points of view,
What you must realize is I am here for you in more ways than one can imagine.

The epic of life exist first in the mind before it becomes real,
Experience of living has shown me what is in my heart should not be concealed.
Secrets misapplied can destroy what is meant to be,
On the outside looking in, it appears to be a mystery.
Many stories not told take on the shape of lies, even when they are true,
This is what happens so often between me and you.

Confusion and chaos sets in,
After so much work we are chasing our tails over and over
again.
The beauty and love of a child is a blessing to embrace,
We must remain free of selfishness not to get lost in the chase
the chase of life that has us all going in circles.
The cycle of life says, "We spend so much of our life looking
forward, but living it backwards"
Our destiny lives through the choices we make or lack there
of.

When one reaches forward to the golden years, will you
look content at a life well lived or appear broken with failed
dreams of living with no purpose.
Now that's a dilemma we all must face.

By making quality decisions in our lives we diminish, but not
erase the hurt and pain of life. We should make decisions
with the consequence and ill effects of what could happen.
Short-term gain with long-term misery is a trap that can be
avoided. Pray, Believe and Act on faith, then you will be free,
free to fly over mountain ranges…smoothly.

Life sometimes teaches us to be gentle, but not the lamb,
Occasionally we must have to look in the mirror and say, "I
think, therefore I am."

Excuse Me while I Reinvent Myself

Ladies and Gentlemen:

I come with a cool approach, a smooth tone kind of light,
but heavy on the side.
Sitting on the deck with thrust in my hands buckle up and
get ready for a ride.

When I started this journey, I vowed to be me,
Staying true to myself, I speak with a limited vocabulary.

But you know, I've seen some things, heard some things that
I am willing to share with you...Life is a Groove.

Facets

Of

Love

Malaysian Heat

It all started in the far eastern sun,
Who would have thought this is where our love begun.
Just the sheer presence of your ecstasy has claimed my being and loyalty.
My arrival to your homeland was strictly business,
I quickly learned what success is.
As you took me in with your family, I was a stranger for all to see.
Such compassion and kindness was shown to me,
I cannot repay what I owe to so many.
In a land not my own, I was lost to find you,
What am I saying?
You found me, too.

The far eastern sun is where it all begun,
To live forever with a taste of the honey that drips from you,
I don't know what I will do without you because in your presence, I stand complete,
In the comfort of my "Malaysian Heat."

My heartbeats with the speed of a race, each time I lose sight of your face.
When we first departed after we met,
I failed to realize what was happening.
I soon understood your place even if I could not adjust to the far eastern pace.
One must absorb the loss of another,
Without feeling sorry for this brother, wait…I feel you. Oh yea…

There it is…now I'm back…
Grooving like a feather in a strong wind, moving back and
forth again and again.

The far eastern sun is where it all begun,
To live forever with a taste of the honey that drips from you,
I don't know what I will do without you because in your
presence, I stand complete,
In the comfort of my "Malaysian Heat."

The length of your legs have got me reaching,
The strength of your love's got me preaching,
About staying together, living forever, seeing the light no
matter what the weather,
The summer is hot, in the spring it rains,
Since we said I do, my life has not been the same.
Feeling you, loving you, holding you, protecting you,
Guiding you to the life I want to share with you…forever.

The far eastern sun is where it all begun,
To live forever with a taste of the honey that drips from you,
I don't know what I will do without you because in your
presence, I stand complete,
In the comfort of my "Malaysian Heat."

I hit the lottery by making you my wife.
We walk down the street, receiving stares,
I don't mind, nor do I even care.
We aspire to have more, but as long as we have each other,
We will never be hungry.
I can feed on you through eternity.

In Awe of You

It seems my whole life has been a tailspin,
All I do is go in circles searching for you,
In the sun, in the rain, in the eye of a storm,
Reaching through the fog and in the mist of the morning
dew.
My heart aches for what it does not have, because I always
feel you with me,
Evolution brings life, but without you I cannot see.
Blind to the elements of this world is a lonely place,
It's funny how I am full of life with you in my space.
The choices I have made have gotten me where I am,
Sitting and wondering is my affection a scam to deceive me
and have me vulnerable to who I am.

If I sound confused, it's because it's true,
I am caught up, in awe of you.

Captured by the curves of your presence, you stop traffic
with the sound of your voice,
You can also make one want to drive fast, regardless of their
choice.
You are love, happiness, sadness and joy all wrapped into one,
You are the center of my universe, like planets moving
around the sun.

I close my eyes to feel your groove,
Whether you are here or not I want to move.
Your style changes and remains the same,

You demand respect with little time for games.
I struggle within my heart trying to adjust to you,
God please help me, I don't know what to do.

If I sound confused, it's because it's true,
I am caught up, in awe of you.

I am trying to embrace this joy inside,
Lord knows I don't want to go for a ride… To a place
abandoned in the shadows.
In awe of you,
I exist to love what we are together,
It does not matter; I accept we will make this forever.
I love you and I believe you are an entity connected to my
soul,
You are country, classical, rhythm and blues also rock and
roll.

I must embrace the joy that I feel,
No matter what happens I know this is real.
I am here for you to see this through with no end in sight,
I want to love you both day and night.
To feel beats in constant motion,
With a harmonic groove covered in the soft lotion…of love.
If I sound confused, it's because it's true,
I am caught up, in awe of you.

I thought I penetrated you to release myself,
I am not here to simply attain wealth.
I am alive and well with the melodies we create,
I know you do this to others, but are the results of a similar
fate.

I love what you do to me please don't stop,
Busting me with expression from the bottom to the top.

Lady music groove with me
I am yours, groove with me.

Fragrance of Life

As I close my eyes I imagine the smell of your perfume,
I sit and fantasize about the privacy of being in your room.
The scent that surrounds you cannot be bought in a store,
It is the fragrance of your body that keeps me coming back
for more.
What will you have me do to, absorb your every need,
To be there in times of failure, in addition, when you
succeed.
I have no urge to control or tell you what to do,
But when you need strength I will stand for you.
Please understand we will be together for sure,
In a world full of change, you are forever mi amore.
I believe we are meant to be, will you fulfill my destiny,
A friend, lover, playmate and wife,
I will protect, love and nourish your fragrance of life.

Senseless is what I am about you,
What's amazing is you show me so much love too.
My reflection in the mirror is no longer alone,
Together as one we have grown…to ecstasy, dutifully,
meaningfully, lovingly, intensely, not holding back, but
holding on to what may sustain us through eternity.

Oh this is suppose to be an illustration of love…
Please understand we will be together for sure,
In a world full of change, you are forever mi amore.
I believe we are meant to be, will you fulfill my destiny,
A friend, lover, playmate and wife,
I will protect, love and nourish your fragrance of life.

Safe is what I am when we are together,
A merry go-round of love no matter what the weather.
I ease through my day with you on my mind,
Is your reflection of me of a similar kind?
I am losing myself in you again and again,
To regain composure after you say when.
Have you had enough? Do you want more?
Tell me to stop or have you had it this way before.
I don't mind taking you there to that place,
You know where you forget time and space.
Please understand we will be together for sure,
In a world full of change, you are forever mi amore.
I believe we are meant to be, will you fulfill my destiny,
A friend, lover, playmate and wife,
I will protect, love and nourish your fragrance of life.
The pain of your absence I don't want to understand,
Please help me to reach that sacred place with you, not for a
moment but forever,
Just say when.

Icy Hot

It started with a glare that stopped me in my tracks,
Your mere presence had hit me just like that,
For some time you did not know me,
The heat of attraction would bring us to be,
I noticed you while in the work place,
By which it appeared we had similar taste.
In a world full of change I made a choice,
What got my attention further was the sound of your voice,
Between our ages was so much time, but I could not resist
the curves and lines,
Of your body.
Fresh with the essence of baby's milk and skin so smooth, it
was woven silk.
When you were quiet and out of touch for me to see,
It was your body that talked to me.

I said you were in my heart,
And that was the line to break it all apart.
Through all the fun and discussions we had,
It's a shame we left each other mad at the web we created
I did not know when to stop,
I know without a doubt you are Icy Hot.

Hot to the touch and sweet to the smell,
Soft with the lips with a promise not to tell,
Of the ice in your veins and the coldness in your heart,
Finally to end something you wanted to start.
No need to blame me now, occasionally, I wonder why you
remained quiet,
In the end you could not stay silent.
You said I burned the candle at both ends,
You got the firmness until you said when… And them some
Move in with me was the bait you used,
To determine who would win or lose,
You said I kept secrets to be won,
In the end we both know you kept a bigger one.
I did not know when to stop,
I know without a doubt you are Icy Hot.

Hot to the touch and sweet to the smell,
Soft with the lips with a promise not to tell,
Of the ice in your veins and the coldness in your heart,
Finally to end something you wanted to start.
No need to blame me now, occasionally, I wonder why you
remained quiet,
In the end you could not stay silent.
It's too damn cold in Boston, Goodbye.

Seasons Change

As I wake to the morning dew,
I spread my wings with everlasting thoughts of you,
It is such a wonder how you affect me,
As I gaze in the eastern sky patiently,
Thoughts of you remain still, but I have to accept time will
continue.
It is the summer sun with heat soon to follow,
Will this time remain or will the time stay the same.
As the world turns, it evolves around the sun; I never wanted
to hurt anyone,
If there is one thing I have learned, nothing remains the
same.
Seasons Change.

You laughed and mocked me from the start,
When we met, I thought I would be in your heart.
It's odd considering what you said to my face,
Now realizing you did not want me in any case.
It's amazing the mask I could not see through,
I really believed I loved you.
The game of love was a way of capturing me,
Until a child unborn, never got a chance to see.
Selfishly everyone got blamed except you,
The shame of it all lies in the fact you fooled your own
reflection in the mirror.

In the fall season full of color you camouflaged your identity.
How long can you hide who you really are?
As the world turns, it evolves around the sun; I never wanted
to hurt anyone,
If there is one thing I have learned, nothing remains the
same.
Seasons Change.

As cold as it is outside, it is better than lying next to you in
here,
The heat of your body has been released to the atmosphere.
It was never meant for me, and now I see.
I can't miss what I never had; so glad I have not gone insane.
The pain of a bad choice is what affects me most,
Clearly I now see what is just a ghost of my imagination.
I do hurt…my God its cold beside you.
As the world turns, it evolves around the sun; I never wanted
to hurt anyone,
If there is one thing I have learned, nothing remains the
same.
Seasons Change.

Once again I spread my wings, prepared to jump off the
rooftops,
It was certain death so I thought.
To my surprise the wind provided lift to fly high in the sky.
Today I stand with power in my hands,
Without you I walk through the meadows.

A child was taken without cause,
But I live on with the memory not lost.
The spring brings life and I will go without malice and strife.

I hear birds singing from the trees,
The morning dew is fresh to start a new day.
As the world turns, it evolves around the sun; I never wanted
to hurt anyone,
If there is one thing I have learned, nothing remains the
same.
Seasons Change and so do people.

Djenaba

When I laid my eyes on what beauty God gave you my heart
stood still,
To this day I wonder what could have been if only your will
was out of my way.
Your mind could not overcome what your eyes would see,
In the mist of so much vanity you could not find the best in
me.
Why is it, we want what we don't need,
All I wanted with you has become lost to time indeed.
I stumbled with you when I should have stood still,
Now as I reflect on history, the heat has since chilled by my
own decisions.
I stare into the night knowing you are not looking back at
me,
Invisible to you, I would never get and opportunity to reveal
myself.
In a world full of dreams, life brings about reality,
I have lost what I never had in you,
Maybe I would feel better if you thought of me too.
I miss what I never had in us,
But still I live to love another day,
It's funny, but have you ever thought of me in this way?

You move on and I go around starting over again,
Our choices have shown me what I should have known back
when.
I did not want to believe you could not see through to my
heart,

I was clearly unseen from the start.
In the chess game of life what are we to do,
It seems I have missed my chance at you.

This is not a sad story at all,
Just something for you to know, I moved too slow when
I should have kicked the door in to open my passion and
groove with the movement of your soul to give all that I am
and release all that I have…an explosion of the strength that
comes with the joy of knowing I am the one to hold onto…
Damn, too little too late will teach me not to hesitate,
Djenaba you have no idea.

In a world full of dreams, life brings about reality,
I have lost what I never had in you,
Maybe I would feel better if you thought of me too.
I miss what I never had in us,
But still I live to love another day,
It's funny, but have you ever thought of me in this way?

The Voice Of A Woman

Your beauty is only paralleled by your voice and,
It takes only a moment to reflect a bad choice.

Though I live based on my own decisions,
I find myself lost without the precision
(Of your wisdom)

The expressions of your love are constantly shown to me,
This only illustrates the strength of your integrity.

You willingly give me the experience of your lifetime,
And I openly submit not wanting to be left behind,
Due to the ignorance of my youth.

Boldly you tell me what I need to hear time and time again,
Still I give in once in a while to sin.

Fighting to protect what I love the most,
Over and over you remind me to coast,
Through the process of life and not to be too eager.

I live for a purpose I do not fully understand,
It is so unclear as to my ultimate plan.
With your love, strength and elegance, you encourage me to
stand.

Whether I sleep, push to excel or monitor what I eat,
Your voice constantly reminds me I am in the driver's seat.

Maybe you can tell me where I am going and how far,
To date I am still reaching for that star.

You always lift me up, even when I'm not down,
That's why I give you this crown,
I place on you forever.

I love who you are to me.
Your voice is the essence of my power and we are just getting
started.

Talk to me woman, Talk to me!

Your voice so sweet to the touch keeps me warm at night,
even in your absence.
Your voice strips me of the garments that hide my manhood.

And it is your voice that brings me back stronger than before,
every time.

Talk to me woman, Talk to me!

The

Other

Side

The Devil's Deal

It all started many years ago when I was a child,
Running through the park playing for a while,
Enjoying the sun and the noon day heat,
Exhausting myself until it was time to eat.
Through the shadows she appeared pretty with curly hair,
Smiling while I would jut stare.
All she wanted was to be my playmate,
After days, weeks and months we would not separate.
Many times she asked to have me,
So young and naïve I did not know she wanted eternity.
In the mist of trying to be wise,
I never knew she was the devil in disguise.
Is this fiction or is this real?
I know nothing of the devil's deal.

I get older and learn a little about life,
Each day comes with more challenge,
I do my best to keep things in check,
While I balance school and athletics.
I enjoy the attention from success at an early age,
As I prepared to make the world my stage.

This time it comes in the form of adulation and praise,
It is intoxicating to receive so much attention early in life,
The temptation was the mark of strife.
I tried to accept it with grace,
But everyday I ran a race to out perform myself.
In the mist of trying to be wise,

I never knew popularity would be the devil in disguise.
Is this fiction or is this real?
I know nothing of the devil's deal.

I mature into manhood to realize my dreams,
Fall in love, get married or so it seemed.
The wrong choice in a mate can bring pain,
Through the entire mess, why go insane?
Heartbreak is one thing, but divorce is another,
I did not want to be a statistic like other brothers.
The sorrow was sinking deep like quicksand,
Making me weak instead of a strong man.
A lonely man I considered the choices I would make,
As I move forward what will it take?

In the mist of trying to be wise,
I never knew loneliness could be the devil in disguise.
Is this fiction or is this real?
I know nothing of the devil's deal.

As one who has lived and enjoyed this place,
I look around at what I face.
I look around at what means a lot, my family, friends and
relationships through the years,
The ones I have lost at times bring me to tears.
I read, meditate and pray constantly,
Without God's love where would I be?
You see through the years, I have learned the devil wants me,
In many ways he tries so diligently.

One night in a dream I heard a voice,
I was forced to listen without a choice.
It said, for many years I have followed you around,
Now I have a deal you cannot turn down.
All the people you love, your family and friends,
I have peace for you until the very end.
If you give me you and worship darkness in all that you do,
Those you love will be free to do as they choose too.
I was confused by this attempt for me,
Do I keep my soul or agree.
I love my family and friends more than gold,
Do I attempt to save them and give away my soul?
The devil promised to leave them alone you see,
All I had to do was give him me.
In the mist of trying to be wise,
I never knew a deal would be the devil in disguise,
Is this fiction or is this real?
I know nothing of the devil's deal.

Could I save my family…or is that even my responsibility?
I reached my hands to the sky and asked God to please help
me.
In my meekness…the devil has found my weakness.
I have been taught to protect those I love,
But I need you to protect me from above.
Lord, guard my thoughts and guard my actions,
The devil is trying to provoke a reaction.
I need to make a divine correction, to reflect and make the
right selection.

If you were given this choice to make,
What path would you take?
Do I try to protect my family?
Or do I leave them to the powers that be.
If this proposal was to you…what exactly would you do?
Never make a deal with the devil in any way,
Yea right,
Most of us compromise ourselves everyday.

I am so challenged by this…God help me.

Staring into Darkness

I look into the sky amazed by what I see,
Not knowing the reality of what is before me,
At times, it's colors that get my attention,
On occasion I do not understand the layers I am in.
The blue illuminates with a cleanliness that is clear,
As deep as I gaze, not able to measure what is far or near.
I use to believe for it to be true,
The measure of clarity was in the color blue.
As soon as I accepted that bad information,
The sky gave me more colors for interpretation.
Red expressed deeply within my heart,
Moments of intensity as it appeared at the start of a new day.
Certain times I see it at dusk,
This I do not understand, but the feeling is associated with
lust.
Orange and yellow also comes through,
With these colors I am lost with what to do.

Many emotions surface within my soul,
I focus sometimes though…always reaching for a goal.
Purple in the sky is what causes the most concern,
I have yet to realize what I am to learn from the haze.
The creativity flows like the Nile,
Do I sit or move based on what is in style.

It's funny how we move forward, but usually end up living
backwards,
As the past is sure to re-surface itself if it's not given its due

respect and attention.
What maintains a grip on me is the stillness of the night,
It is the darkness that reveals the light within us
I often wonder who or what is looking at me,
As I stare in the darkness of destiny.
Is it real, is it alive or dead,
The darkness moves ever so slowly and reflects on what life
force it's fed.

The stars shine ever so brightly most of the time,
Even when I cannot see them, they exist within my mind.
My sense of stability comes from what I see in the darkness,
It is a miracle to have learned this lesson.
You see the darkness does not only exist in the night,
Whenever my will dims the light that glows within me,
I must stand and not be afraid of the darkness that stares
right back.

Support

And

Encouragement

Mother Annie Mae

When I started this I opened up my heart,
Though I should have known this right from the start,
So young I was to begin this with ambition,
Constantly working to focus on my mission,
I should have been listening to you from birth,
Since you have always been a part of me here on earth.
Do as you're told, mind your manners and treat others as you
want to be treated is what you would say to me,
In shame and disgust I admit I listened rarely.
I wasn't bad or good, often…
I did as I thought I should,
The legacy you have left, I now understand,
Approach life with a kind heart and helping hand.
Without a shadow of doubt, I know you are in heaven with
God above,
Looking upon us all sending your love.
You gave so much to ask for nothing at all,
That is the greatest compliment I have to offer, as I stand tall.
The challenge I have for me, and all of you,
Is to live you life, but think of Mother Annie Mae too.

Just imagine, living your life getting in the environment and
have everyone knowing you are at heaven's door,
Beyond, degrees, money, fancy clothes and cars, that's the
recognition I want to strive for.
When I move on from this world, what would others say?
Does it matter…would we all be in heaven with Mother
Annie Mae?

I challenge myself and I challenge you too,
Submit yourself to the proper cause to love and kind, like
Mother Annie Mae would do.
So instead if standing in this world so tall,
We can all be with God smiling like Mother Annie Mae
Rawls.

In the Middle

Before I arrived she stood waiting with malice, but with concern and never hesitating;
She saw what many refused to see.
She even went where many did not go,
Small in stature but strong in mind,
She presents a unique kind of girl that could only be overlooked if you closed your heart to what brilliance your eyes could not see.

Then I came into this world wondering who this girl was and what she thought about me.
In my innocence I followed her joyfully to explore her surroundings while ignoring my own.
I never meant to intrude, though usually, I ended up annoying her with my presence.
If only she knew all this time,
Her strength to endure has been an inspiration to lift my dreams into reality.

I was followed by youth, focus and stubbornness combined with a face which I call her today.
I believed it was my job to lead the way into the abyss,
With lessons of life at hand our priorities would change in the order of our need for guidance; though our birth dates remained the same.
In trying to lead I found my place in the middle of those who watch out for me.

It's funny how we joke about being born,
With people getting busted up at the Capricorn.
I have been protecting to learn I need to have my own
perimeter guarded against those with no motive more than a
lack of desire to earn while using lies, deception and trickery
to find a way to get ahead.

Thank you, my sisters …

In the mist of my bad choices, you never gave up on me and
I refuse to give up on you.

Much love,
Your Brother

Layers

The start of life begins as a seed; watered, fertilized, or cultivated, it is truly what we need.

As we begin so pure from the start, we move forward with influences penetrating our heart.

It comes patient and slow, quick then fast.
It surrounds us entirely; in addition, it may last, longer than expected.

It's invisible, but on occasion we can see it.

It can be insulation, also protection from the elements.

They come in pieces, maybe whole, sometimes thick, other times thin.
It's sad how we cover up from being naked to ourselves due to the world we live in.

Layers, good or bad, smother's the truth when what should be revealed lives within all of us.

Layers, cold or hot, hides the truth of what we are feeling when we cannot explain our emotions.

Layers, plenty or few, covers the truth to cause the most harm to those we love, though we convince ourselves we are protecting them.

Layers, hard or soft, distort the truth as we refuse to allow our purity to be seen as we cover it with corrupt information.

Layers, thick or thin, bury the truth and choke our spirit until it is barely alive.

We move forward through life attracting what we think we want with little understanding of what we need.

We lie to ourselves attracting the mask of our experiences.

It's funny, no; it's dangerous to believe what we are not.

Constantly dreaming ignoring the reality of what we are living.

Dreaming is healthy when we find, discover, and connect the abyss with reality.

What a beautiful world it would be to reflect on our nakedness without the chaos and confusion of *Layers*, placed on us through the distortion of history, media, allies, enemies, judges, lawyers, politicians and certain religious leaders that seek to serve themselves by using the labor of unsuspecting people.

To remove *layers*, good and bad, releases the truth to reveal the sincerity that lives within us.

To remove *layers*, cold or hot, uncovers the truth of our emotions to show how we feel.

To remove *layers*, plenty or few, unleashes the truth to protect those we love thereby saving them from harm of those seeking ill gotten gain.

To remove *layers*, hard or soft, clarifies the truth as we provide clear information to illustrate what remains pure in each of us.

To remove *layers*, thick or thin, creates life in truth which builds perseverance and strength in our spirit.

The world and those with an ulterior motive continues to push *layers* upon us to conform to a standard that constantly attempts to subject us under their authority to be manipulated.

Well, as for me, I will choose my own destiny.

I choose to live BUTT ASS NAKED.

And you, what do you choose?

The Man Within

That which embodies my soul I do not understand,
It evolves within, to create a strong man.

There are so many ingredients that contribute to making this
dish,
A prayer; to HIM who listens while simultaneously living on
a wish.

What or who can manifest a boy into manhood,
As I learn not to become a victim of being misunderstood.

Mere thoughts of righteousness, perseverance, strength,
honesty, independence, tenacity, love and a willingness to
face adversity must be converted into action,
To talk without substance is a worst attraction.

Is it easy to sit and do nothing but watch others give?
With maturity we learn if our thoughts are not turned into
action we become docile and ineffective.

One treasure in life is to explore and discover this Man
Within,
Is he real, does he exist, am I going in circles just to begin
again.

I look in the mirror and what do I see,
More times than not; a reflection of many people looking
back at me.

The more I seek to look inside of this person the more
confused I become,
The good I do at times is countered by bad thoughts, this is
so cumbersome.

I seldom speak, but when I do it's important to remember
what's said,
As some choose to distort my words.

One treasure in life is to explore and discover this Man
Within,
Is he real, does he exist, am I going in circles just to begin
again.

My dear child, you are flesh of my flesh which I have put
into print,
Remember life is a marathon, but certainly not a sprint.

With no knowledge or awareness of my grandfather's
contributions to me,
I had to rely only on what I could see.

I was blinded by the brightness of the glow,
In the end I learned there is still so much more to know.

Thankfully my father filled the gaps for me,
I am grateful beyond calculation as I measure up to who I am
to be.

As I physically become weaker,
You become stronger,
As I spiritually and intellectually become stronger,

I will empower you with the knowledge and wisdom to apply it correctly.

Therefore you must listen, understand and move forward with precise aggression.

One treasure in life is to explore and discover this Man Within,
Is he real, does he exist, am I going in circles just to begin again.

I don't know how, what or when,
But I must unleash this Man Within.

I can no longer be silent; I must stand and shout,
I must go in deeply to allow this Man Within to find HIS way out.

And

The

Saga

Continues...

Volume II will reveal itself in years to come.

The word of God makes it clear to be alert, cautious
and active.
(1 Peter 5:8)
We are to fan the flame and stir up the gifts within us.
(2 Timothy 1:6)

The metal iron is full of impurities that weaken it; through
forging, it becomes steel and is transformed into a razor-
sharp sword. Human beings develop in the same fashion.
Morikei Ueshiba

Remember, to surround yourself with individuals who will
help to enable your courage when it is lacking.
Coach K

Then, rests satisfied with doing well and leave others to talk
of you as they please.
Pythagoras

Don't worry about anything instead pray about everything.
Tell God what you need, and thank Him for all He has done.
If you do this you will experience God's peace,
This is far more wonderful than the human mind can
understand.
(Philippians 4:6-7)

About the Author

Freddie McSears Jr. who solely authored this is a God fearing man. He is a father, author, educator, friend, accountant, bass guitar player, professional airline pilot, cook, son, brother, uncle and artist of life.

He holds a Master's degree from the University of Central Michigan. His undergraduate studies were completed at Delaware State University. He also wrote, "Broken Wings a Strong Heart." He is currently working on his most controversial literary piece. One can expect him to not hide behind the truth, but to reveal his truth. In addition, he continues to work on his music.

Creating and learning about music, jogging and walks on a beach; various physical activities and hosting dinners are among his leisure activities. He has a reputation of being quite a cook.

COVER DESIGN AND ILLUSTRATION BY MIKE BENNETT www.mikebennettgraghics.com